*To my dear aunt, Pat Wallace, a woman
of kindness, patience, and faith*

Contents

Acknowledgments

I WOULD LIKE TO THANK Stephanie Bowen, senior editor at Sourcebooks, for approving and supporting this project and Jeff Smith for his editorial assistance. Gratitude also goes to Grace Menary-Winefield for her work on this new edition.

Introduction

WHEN YOU SIT DOWN AND think about the Bible's impact on our world and on human history, it's really no surprise that you are taking time to read this book of Bible trivia. After all, the Bible is the bestselling book of all time, so by understanding it better, you can also understand and appreciate the unspoken influence it has on our everyday lives.

There is no way of knowing exactly how many Bibles have been sold and distributed worldwide ever since the first Bible was printed on a Gutenberg press over 550 years ago, though publishers estimate that six billion copies have been purchased over the years. By contrast, Harry Potter, the all-time bestselling book series, has sold 450 million copies, making it a very distant second to a book commonly described as the story of God's love and pursuit of humankind.

Just how popular is the Bible? Consider the following:

- More than 100 million copies are sold globally each year, and countless others are distributed for free in open and closed countries.

- The Scriptures have been translated into more than 500 languages, and another 2,300 languages have had at least a portion of the Bible translated into that language.
- For centuries, countless men and women have committed their lives and even died in order to translate, distribute, smuggle, and teach the Bible to thousands of groups around the world.
- Even in the United States, more than 160,000 copies are sold or given away each day.

So what fuels this unparalleled hunger for, and devotion to, the so-called good book? There are lots of theories, but for most of us, it really comes down to the Bible's proven track record for changing lives. Millions (if not billions) of people in nearly every country of the world claim that the Bible's teachings have transformed their hearts and altered their values and their way of thinking about life for the better. Some had the Bible taught to them when they were young children. Others discovered the Bible's message of hope, faith, and love in the midst of a personal crisis or as seekers on a spiritual journey.

So why have you come to this book, and how will it enhance your understanding and appreciation of the Bible? Perhaps you want to get to know God more intimately—or for the first time—through the pages of Scripture. Maybe you have unanswered questions or concerns about the Bible's truth claims. Or you might be "dipping your toe in the water" again after growing up in the church and then falling away.

No matter your situation, after reading this book and taking the simple quizzes created for each of the books of the Bible, you will come away with a stronger understanding of Scripture. If you don't regularly read the Bible, I believe this trivia book will prepare you to begin enjoying this one-of-a-kind book on your own. For those of you who are just beginning to read the Bible for yourself, I suggest you start with Genesis, the first book of the Bible, and then proceed with the book of John in the New Testament, found about two-thirds of the way into the Bible, before delving into other Bible books. By doing this, you'll learn the basic facts about the Bible, find out how the books are divided into Old Testament and New Testament sections, and receive a high-level introduction to all Old Testament and New Testament tomes.

If you are already a regular Bible reader, you'll notice that these quizzes together do not form a comprehensive survey of the Bible, nor are they intended to. Instead, the questions in this book—which primarily use the English Standard Version translation of Scripture—are intended to test your knowledge of the Bible's highlights and give you a greater appreciation for the Bible's depth and God's relationship with and love for humankind. You can take the quizzes in this book in whatever order you wish, though you may find it most beneficial to work through them chronologically, starting with Genesis and ending with Revelation, or to go straight to the sections that you may have struggled with most or may not recall as well as others.

By the time you complete the quiz for the book of Revelation, you'll have met many of the fascinating kings, prophets, disciples, and men and women of God that you and I can credit for providing and preserving the Bible for our enjoyment and development. Perhaps someday you'll look back and see the Bible's impact on your own life and join the ever-growing list of people whose lives have been changed by Scripture's unchanging truth.

JAMES STUART BELL

General Bible Questions

1. How many books are in the Bible?
   a. 47
   b. 55
   c. 66
   d. 70

2. How many books are in the Old Testament?
   a. 37
   b. 39
   c. 41
   d. 43

3. How many books are in the New Testament?
   a. 24
   b. 25
   c. 26
   d. 27

4. What is the shortest book of the Bible?
    a. Obadiah
    b. Malachi
    c. Philemon
    d. 3 John

5. What is the longest book in the Bible?
    a. Jeremiah
    b. Psalms
    c. Isaiah
    d. Genesis

6. What is the shortest book of the Old Testament?
    a. Ruth
    b. Obadiah
    c. Haggai
    d. Zephaniah

7. What is the longest book of the New Testament?
    a. Luke
    b. Acts
    c. Matthew
    d. Revelation

8. How many chapters are in the entire Bible?
   a. 587
   b. 898
   c. 1,189
   d. 1,667

9. Which of the following books contains the Ten Commandments?
   a. Genesis
   b. Leviticus
   c. Deuteronomy
   d. Numbers

10. Which three books are referred to as the Major Prophets?
   a. Isaiah, Jeremiah, and Ezekiel
   b. Isaiah, Daniel, and Jonah
   c. Jeremiah, Hosea, and Malachi
   d. Jeremiah, Daniel, and Nehemiah

11. Which five Old Testament books are considered wisdom literature or poetry?
   a. Ruth, Esther, Psalms, Proverbs, and Song of Solomon
   b. Leviticus, Ezra, Proverbs, Ecclesiastes, and Habakkuk
   c. Psalms, Proverbs, Song of Solomon, Lamentations, and Daniel
   d. Job, Psalms, Proverbs, Ecclesiastes, and Song of Solomon

12. Which Old Testament book does not mention God?
    a. Ruth
    b. Esther
    c. Song of Solomon
    d. Zephaniah

13. What is the correct order of the gospels (the first four books of the New Testament)?
    a. Mark, Matthew, Luke, John
    b. Matthew, Mark, Luke, John
    c. Matthew, Mark, John, Luke
    d. Mark, Matthew, John, Luke

14. How many letters of the New Testament did the apostle Paul author?
    a. 9
    b. 11
    c. 13
    d. 16

15. The four authors responsible for writing multiple New Testament books are Paul, Peter, John, and Matthew.
    True
    False

16. Which book is considered the wisdom literature of the New Testament?
    a. James
    b. Revelation
    c. Acts
    d. Galatians

17. Which gospel contains Jesus's Sermon on the Mount?
    a. Matthew
    b. Mark
    c. Luke
    d. John

18. How many verses are found in Jesus's teaching in the Sermon on the Mount?
    a. 107
    b. 144
    c. 76
    d. 201

19. Which Old Testament book prophesied that Jesus would be born in Bethlehem?
    a. Malachi
    b. Daniel
    c. Isaiah
    d. Micah

20. How many times is the word "Immanuel" mentioned in the Bible?
    a. 1
    b. 3
    c. 7
    d. 10

21. The Bible claims to be the divinely inspired, errorless word of God.
    True
    False

22. The Old Testament has _____ total chapters.
    a. 818
    b. 929
    c. 1,004
    d. 1,005

23. The Bible is the world's most translated book.
    True
    False

24. The New Testament has _____ total chapters.
    a. 260
    b. 270
    c. 280
    d. 290

25. The wisdom books of the Bible are Job, Psalms, Proverbs, Ecclesiastes, and Song of Solomon.

    True

    False

26. Which of the following is not one of the prophets' books?

    a. Isaiah

    b. Lamentations

    c. Daniel

    d. Ezra

27. Acts is the book that covers the history of the early church.

    True

    False

28. What is the last word of the Bible (found in Revelation 22:21)?

    a. You

    b. Christ

    c. Amen

    d. Forever

29. Jude and Philemon are the apocalypse (final events) books of the Bible.

    True

    False

30. How many times does the name "God" appear in the King James version of the Bible?
    a. 2,908
    b. 3,358
    c. 4,473
    d. 7,193

General Bible Answer Key

1. C
2. B
3. D
4. D
5. B
6. B
7. A
8. C
9. C
10. A
11. D
12. B
13. B
14. C
15. False (Luke is the fourth author.)
16. A
17. A
18. A

19. D
20. B
21. True
22. B
23. True
24. A
25. False (The wisdom books provide special spiritual insight into the nature of God, people, suffering, and a walk with God.)
26. D
27. True
28. C
29. False (Final events refers to the last days of life as we currently know it here on earth, including the second coming of Christ to take Christians to heaven.)
30. B

Old Testament Questions

⊛ GENESIS

1. Eve was created from which part of Adam's body?
   a. heart
   b. leg
   c. rib
   d. brain

2. In what order did God create the elements of the universe?
   a. the heavens and the earth; day and night; land and vegetation; fish and birds; sun, moon, and stars; land animals
   b. day and night; sun, moon, and stars; sky and sea; fish and birds; land and vegetation; land animals
   c. sky and sea; day and night; sun, moon, and stars; land and vegetation; fish and birds; land animals
   d. day and night; sky and sea; land and vegetation; sun, moon, and stars; birds and fish; land animals

3. What did God put into the nostrils of Adam that made him alive?

    a. the air of animation

    b. the wind of power

    c. the blood of God

    d. the breath of life

4. God commanded Adam and Eve to eat only from the tree of the knowledge of good and evil in the Garden of Eden.

    True

    False

5. What classic phrase begins the serpent's speech to Eve in his scheme to get her to sin?

    a. "Thou shalt not covet…"

    b. "Do you want to be like God?"

    c. "Did God really say…"

    d. "All these I will give you…"

6. What did Adam and Eve sew together to cover themselves after they realized they were naked in the Garden of Eden?

    a. animal skins

    b. fig leaves

    c. pieces of cloth

    d. palm branches

7. What two things did God put outside the Garden of Eden to block the way to the tree of life?
    a. a gate and a guard
    b. a maze and a river
    c. an angel and a sword
    d. a sphinx and a chasm

8. Adam and Eve's first two sons were Cain and Abel.
    True
    False

9. What food item did Cain present to the Lord as an offering?
    a. fruits of the soil
    b. vegetables
    c. meat
    d. fat

10. What does God say to Cain about sin?
    a. that it stalks him in the field
    b. that it is deep within his heart
    c. that it is breathing down his neck
    d. that it is crouching at his door

11. Which descendant of Adam had the longest mortal life in the Bible, and how many years did he live?
    a. Mahalalel, 895 years
    b. Sherupalel, 1,046 years
    c. Enosh, 905 years
    d. Methuselah, 969 years

12. Who of the following was not one of Noah's three sons?
    a. Sham
    b. Joseph
    c. Ham
    d. Japheth

13. Why did God decide to flood the earth in Noah's time?
    a. Because of the evil of men that covered the earth
    b. To scatter the people to different places
    c. To save the animals from being destroyed by men
    d. Because global temperatures were getting too high

14. How many days did the great flood last?
    a. 6
    b. 40
    c. 80
    d. 150

15. How old was Noah when the great flood began?

    a. 60

    b. 160

    c. 330

    d. 600

16. After the flood, what was the sign of the covenant between God and humankind that he would never again destroy the world with a flood?

    a. a sacrificial lamb

    b. a dove

    c. a rainbow

    d. a burning bush

17. In what land was the Tower of Babel built?

    a. Shinar

    b. Geshbon

    c. Terah

    d. Egypt

18. What did God do to the people who were building the Tower of Babel so they would not try to build a tower to heaven again?

    a. confused their language and dispersed them

    b. struck them down with fire

    c. turned them into pillars of salt

    d. made them all blind

19. God told _____ that he would make a great nation from him and cause his descendants to be as numerous as the stars.
    a. Noah
    b. Abraham
    c. Adam
    d. Joseph

20. How old were Abraham and Sarah when Sarah became pregnant with their first child?
    a. 80 and 70
    b. 90 and 80
    c. 100 and 90
    d. 110 and 100

21. What was the name of Abraham and Sarah's first child?
    a. Isaac
    b. Jacob
    c. Esau
    d. Joseph

22. Jacob tricked his brother, Esau, out of his _____.
    a. money
    b. cattle
    c. buried treasure
    d. birthright

23. Joseph's brothers sold him into slavery. How many brothers did Joseph have?
    a. 10
    b. 11
    c. 12
    d. 13

24. Joseph was thrown into prison because he had an affair with Potiphar's wife.
    True
    False

25. Joseph eventually became Pharaoh's _____.
    a. food taster
    b. second-in-command
    c. slave
    d. friend

26. Joseph's brothers went to Egypt to ask for Joseph's forgiveness.
    True
    False

27. What was discovered in Benjamin's sack of grain?
    a. gold coins
    b. Joseph's silver cup
    c. royal treasure
    d. the queen's jewelry

28. The king of Salem was Melchizedek.
    True
    False

29. God destroyed Sodom and Gomorrah by raining down burning sulfur.
    True
    False

30. Lot's wife turned to sand when she desired to return to Sodom.
    True
    False

✹ EXODUS

1. What was the name of the baby placed in a basket floating in the reeds of the Nile River?
    a. Noah
    b. Joseph
    c. Moses
    d. Aaron

2. The Israelites were forced to gather their own straw to make _____ after Pharaoh became angry with them.
    a. bricks
    b. walls
    c. storehouses
    d. mortar

3. God spoke to Moses on Mount Horeb through a _____.
    a. burning bush
    b. cloud
    c. parted sea
    d. donkey

4. How many commandments did God give to Moses?
    a. 7
    b. 10
    c. 12
    d. 40

5. Where did Moses go to free the Israelites from slavery?
    a. Israel
    b. Judah
    c. Babylon
    d. Egypt

6. Which of the following was not one of the ten plagues cast on Egypt?
    a. locusts
    b. river turned to blood
    c. floods
    d. frogs

7. God parted what body of water to allow the Israelites to escape Pharaoh's army?
    a. Mediterranean Sea
    b. Red Sea
    c. Caspian Sea
    d. Sea of Galilee

8. Moses's staff turned into a snake when he threw it to the ground before Pharaoh.
    True
    False

9. Who was Moses's wife?

    a. Zipporah

    b. Miriam

    c. Rebekah

    d. Sarah

10. God gave Moses the Ten Commandments on Mount

    _____.

    a. Horeb

    b. Olympus

    c. Zion

    d. Sinai

11. Moses's father, Amram, lived to be _____ years old.

    a. 125

    b. 137

    c. 149

    d. 161

12. Aaron was eighty-three and Moses was eighty-two when the men spoke to Pharaoh.

    True

    False

13. The Israelites were slaves in Egypt for _____ years.
    a. 400
    b. 500
    c. 430
    d. 450

14. The first plague cast on Egypt was turning the Nile River into blood.
    True
    False

15. God cursed Egypt with three days of total darkness as one of the ten plagues.
    True
    False

16. Death of the firstborn of each Egyptian family, including Pharaoh's, was the _____ plague on Egypt.
    a. last
    b. first
    c. second
    d. ninth

17. Pharaoh enlisted _____ chariots to capture Moses and the Israelites after freeing them from slavery in Egypt.
    a. 300
    b. 400
    c. 500
    d. 600

18. The first Passover is mentioned in the book of Exodus.
    True
    False

19. The twelve stones on the breastplate of judgment that the high priest wore represented the twelve disciples.
    True
    False

20. What separated the Holy of Holies from the remainder of the tabernacle?
    a. the chief priest
    b. a curtain
    c. a wailing wall
    d. a pillar of clouds

● LEVITICUS

1. What does the word Leviticus mean?
    a. living for God
    b. relating to the Levites
    c. the Lord our God is one
    d. book of life

2. What is Israel instructed not to do about the harvest of fields?
    a. use slaves to gather crops
    b. gather the crops into baskets made of straw
    c. collect the gleanings left over
    d. perform work after sunset

3. Fire consumed _____ sons.
    a. Moses's
    b. Joshua's
    c. Aaron's
    d. Pharaoh's

4. When an Israelite sinned in ignorance, he or she had to make a sacrifice to receive God's forgiveness.
    True
    False

5. The Lord sent fire to consume the first offerings the
   Israelites presented to him in Sinai.
   True
   False

● NUMBERS

1. When did the cloud and fire of the Lord's presence cover the tabernacle?
   a. as a cloud by day and fire by night
   b. whenever the Israelites worshipped God
   c. whenever an enemy was nearby
   d. whenever the people prayed

2. What did the lifting of the cloud of the Lord's presence signify?
   a. that the Israelites were to set out from camp
   b. that the Israelites were to remain at camp
   c. that the Israelites should prepare for battle
   d. that the Israelites should prepare for a feast

3. God instructed Moses to speak to a rock that would yield water to the thirsty Israelites while they wandered the wilderness. What did Moses do instead?
   a. worshipped the rock
   b. struck the rock
   c. condemned the Israelites for their wickedness
   d. cast the rock into the Red Sea

4. How did God react after Moses disobeyed his instructions to speak to the rock that would yield water?
   a. promoted Aaron to lead the Israelites
   b. returned Moses to Egypt
   c. told Moses he would never enter the promised land
   d. made Moses a shepherd again

5. How old did men have to be to go to war for Israel?
   a. 20
   b. 21
   c. 18
   d. 16

6. God asked Moses to present the Reuben tribe before Aaron.
   True
   False

● DEUTERONOMY

1. What is the first of the Ten Commandments?
   a. Thou shalt not murder.
   b. Thou shalt not steal.
   c. Thou shalt not commit adultery.
   d. Thou shalt have no other gods before me.

2. The fourth commandment says to observe the Sabbath day by _____.
   a. refraining from all sin
   b. keeping it holy
   c. worshipping God the entire day
   d. resting from any hint of work

3. The sixth commandment says you shall not commit adultery.
   True
   False

4. The ninth commandment says not to give false testimony against your _____.
   a. neighbor
   b. family
   c. spouse
   d. government

5. The tenth commandment prohibits coveting your neighbor's wife.

   True

   False

6. The promised land was flowing with _____.
   a. milk
   b. priceless jewels
   c. honey
   d. A and C

7. Moses was prohibited from entering the promised land or even seeing it from a distance.

   True

   False

8. By honoring your father and mother, you may _____.
   a. be rich
   b. receive anything you ask for
   c. live long
   d. live prosperously

9. Deuteronomy is the last book of _____.
   a. the Pentateuch
   b. the major prophets
   c. the Talmud
   d. wisdom literature

10. Who wrote Deuteronomy?

    a. Joshua

    b. Aaron

    c. Moses

    d. Gideon

⊛ JOSHUA

1. Whom did Joshua succeed in leading the Israelite people?

    a. Aaron

    b. Abraham

    c. Moses

    d. Isaac

2. Joshua was the son of _____.

    a. Nun

    b. Moses

    c. Samuel

    d. Gershom

3. Rahab hid two spies whom Joshua sent to Jericho.

    True

    False

4. How many times did Joshua and the Israelite army march around Jericho before the city fell to them?

    a. 3

    b. 13

    c. 7

    d. 9

5. When did the Jordan River stop flowing so the Jews could pass over on dry land?
   a. when Joshua slapped the water with his cloak
   b. after the next generation of Jews was baptized
   c. when the walls of Jericho fell into the river
   d. when the feet of those carrying the ark touched the water

6. Joshua's army marched around Jericho for forty days and forty nights before the city fell to them.
   True
   False

⬤ JUDGES

1. Name the judge with thirty sons who had thirty donkeys and who oversaw thirty towns in Gilead.
   a. Jair
   b. Ehud
   c. Caleb
   d. Samson

2. Who was the first judge of Israel?
   a. Caleb
   b. Othniel
   c. Ehud
   d. Deborah

3. God reduced the size of this judge's army from thirty-two thousand soldiers to three hundred but still gave his army victory.
   a. Samson
   b. Ehud
   c. Caleb
   d. Gideon

4. This judge was captured by the Philistines when Delilah shaved off the seven braids of his hair.
   a. Artaxerxes
   b. Jephthah
   c. Samson
   d. Saul

5. Who is the only female judge mentioned in the Bible?
   a. Ruth
   b. Deborah
   c. Hannah
   d. Rebekah

6. Samson tied the tails of four hundred foxes together, set them on fire, and sent them into the Philistines' wheat fields to destroy their crops.
   True
   False

7. Gideon set out a wool fleece at night. If the fleece was dry but the ground was wet in the morning, he knew that God would save Israel from the Midianites.
   True
   False

● RUTH

1. In what biblical period did Ruth's life take place?
    a. Judges
    b. when Israel was united
    c. when Israel was divided
    d. Prophets

2. Ruth's great-grandson was _____.
    a. Saul
    b. David
    c. Solomon
    d. Hezekiah

3. Naomi said, "For where you go, I will go; and where you lodge, I will lodge: your people shall be my people, and your God my God."
    True
    False

4. Naomi's husband was Elimelech.
    True
    False

5. Boaz was Ruth's second husband.
    True
    False

● 1 AND 2 SAMUEL

1. Who is described as "skillful in playing, a man of valor, a man of war, prudent in speech, and a man of good presence, and the Lord is with him"?
   a. Samuel
   b. David
   c. Saul
   d. Samson

2. Who was Samuel's father?
   a. Elkanah
   b. Samson
   c. Gideon
   d. None of the above

3. Who was Samuel's eldest child?
   a. Elkanah
   b. Ehud
   c. Joel
   d. David

4. Why did God remove Saul as king and replace him with David?
   a. David was a man after God's own heart.
   b. Saul rejected the word of the Lord.
   c. Saul was an aging king.
   d. David killed Goliath.

5. How did Saul die?
   a. killed in battle
   b. turned to a pillar of salt
   c. killed by David
   d. suicide

6. David killed Goliath with a sling and two stones.
   True
   False

7. Who of the following was not a child of King David?
   a. Absalom
   b. Tamar
   c. Josiah
   d. Amnon

8. David was the youngest of the sons of _____.
   a. Jesse
   b. Samuel
   c. Saul
   d. Solomon

9. David reigned as king for _____ years.
   a. 30
   b. 40
   c. 50
   d. 60

10. While having an affair with Bathsheba, David sent her husband, Uriah, to the front lines of battle so he would get killed.

True

False

● 1 AND 2 KINGS

1. Elisha cured Naaman of what affliction?

   a. deafness

   b. blindness

   c. leprosy

   d. infertility

2. When two women went to the king's court, each claiming a baby as her own, how did Solomon know which one was the actual mother?

   a. He ordered the women to take a blood test.

   b. He prayed for wisdom.

   c. The real mother was willing to give up the baby so it wouldn't be killed.

   d. The real mother knew the baby's name.

3. Elijah went to heaven via a whirlwind in a chariot of fire.
   True
   False

4. Josiah was _____ years old when he became king of Israel.

   a. 7

   b. 8

   c. 17

   d. 26

5. Besides Elijah, who was the only other person in the Bible never to die?

    a. Enoch

    b. Elisha

    c. Daniel

    d. Malachi

● 1 AND 2 CHRONICLES

1. Who was named king of Judah at age seven?
   a. Jephthah
   b. Josiah
   c. Jehoiada
   d. Joash

2. How many years were God's people in captivity in Babylon?
   a. 70
   b. 100
   c. 50
   d. 80

3. David had a daughter named Tamar.
   True
   False

4. David chose _____ to build the house of the Lord in Israel.
   a. Uzziah
   b. Solomon
   c. Jesse
   d. Absalom

5. King Saul always conferred with God before going
    to battle.
    True
    False

6. Solomon asked God for _____.
    a. wealth
    b. mercy
    c. wisdom
    d. peace

7. Solomon built the temple and the king's palace in twenty
    years.
    True
    False

8. Solomon ruled as Israel's king for fifty years.
    True
    False

✷ EZRA

1. What did King Artaxerxes order?
   a. that the rebuilding of Jerusalem commence
   b. that the Jews use Persian gold and silver for the temple
   c. that the rebuilding of Jerusalem stop
   d. that the temple be built to the gods of Persia

2. What two prophets prophesied to the Jews about resuming the building of the temple?
   a. Haggai and Zechariah
   b. Joel and Hosea
   c. Malachi and Zephaniah
   d. Nahum and Habakkuk

3. Cyrus reigned as Persia's king after Darius.
   True
   False

4. In Ezra 8:24–30, Ezra implored God's blessing on the Jews.
   True
   False

5. In Ezra 10, the Jews finally confessed their sin to God and took an oath before God.
   True
   False

● NEHEMIAH

1. What was Nehemiah's job at the time of Jerusalem's destruction?
    a. chief official
    b. cupbearer to the king
    c. keeper of the king's wardrobe
    d. second-in-command

2. Which king did Nehemiah serve?
    a. Darius
    b. Nebuchadnezzar
    c. Ehud
    d. Artaxerxes

3. Nehemiah organized God's people to _____.
    a. repair the walls of Jerusalem
    b. attack the Ammonites
    c. attack the Ashdodites
    d. rebuild the temple

4. Nehemiah had half of the men reconstructing Jerusalem's walls while the other half held spears, shields, bows, and coats of armor in case an enemy attacked.
    True
    False

5. Nehemiah also led the Jews in renewing their covenant with God.

   True

   False

● ESTHER

1. Who is the queen of Persia at the beginning of the book of Esther?
   a. Susa
   b. Biztha
   c. Vashti
   d. Hadassah

2. Whose name is never mentioned in the book of Esther?
   a. Esther
   b. Mordecai
   c. God
   d. Haman

3. Name the king of Persia in Esther.
   a. Ahasuerus
   b. Haman
   c. Mordecai
   d. Jedidiah

4. Which king selected Esther to be queen of Persia?
   a. Haman
   b. Xerxes
   c. Josiah
   d. Darius

5. As a child, Esther was adopted by her uncle, Mordecai, after her father and mother passed away.

   True

   False

6. What other name did Esther go by?

   a. Susa

   b. Hegai

   c. Abihail

   d. Hadassah

7. Esther risked her life to protect the Jews from the plans of _____ to annihilate them.

   a. Xerxes

   b. Haman

   c. Harbona

   d. Vashti

● JOB

1. Satan asked to test Job's loyalty to God by taking every blessing away from Job. The Lord agreed to put everything in Satan's power except Job's wife.

    True

    False

2. How were Job's children killed?
    a. The Sabeans raided and killed them.
    b. The wind blew their house down on them.
    c. The Chaldeans raided and killed them.
    d. Fire from heaven burned them up.

3. Job heard God speak to him through a _____.
    a. pillar of fire
    b. burning bush
    c. whirlwind
    d. still, small voice

4. When Job's children were killed and his wealth taken away, Job replied by saying _____.
    a. he was born with nothing and he will die with nothing
    b. he had lost all faith in the Lord
    c. blessed be the name of the Lord
    d. A and C

5. Job valued _____ more than anything else in life.
    a. wealth
    b. family
    c. status
    d. the word of the Lord

6. Shadrach, Meshach, and Abednego comforted Job in his suffering.
   True
   False

7. Job lived in the land of Uz.
   True
   False

● PSALMS

1. Who authored most of Psalms?
   a. Solomon
   b. David
   c. Paul
   d. None of the above

2. Psalm 119:105 says, "Thy word is a lamp unto my feet and a light unto my _____."
   a. heart
   b. path
   c. eyes
   d. walk

3. Psalm 119 is the longest chapter in the Bible.
   True
   False

4. Psalm 23 opens with "The Lord is my _____, I shall not want."
   a. God
   b. savior
   c. shepherd
   d. redeemer

5. Psalm 23 ends with "…and I shall dwell in the house of the Lord _____."
   a. my God
   b. forever
   c. restoring my soul
   d. all the days of my life

6. Psalm 119:11 says the author has hidden God's word in his heart that he might not sin against God.
   True
   False

7. Psalm 19 says the _____ declare the glory of God.
   a. angels
   b. heavens
   c. people
   d. lilies

8. Psalm 20:7 says that some trust in chariots and some trust in horses, but God's people trust in the name of the Lord our God.
   True
   False

9. David implored God to forgive and forget the _____ of David's youth.

    a. failures

    b. laziness

    c. sordid past

    d. sins

10. According to Psalm 21:9, those who commit evil will someday face judgment.

    True

    False

● PROVERBS

1. Solomon wrote most of Proverbs.
   True
   False

2. Proverbs 1:7 says, "The fear of the Lord is the beginning of _____."
   a. wisdom
   b. understanding
   c. knowledge
   d. friendship

3. Proverbs 3:5 says to "Trust in the Lord with all your heart, soul, mind, and strength."
   True
   False

4. Solomon is considered one of Scripture's wisest men.
   True
   False

5. Proverbs 3:12 says that for whom the Lord loves, he _____.
   a. blesses
   b. strengthens
   c. protects
   d. corrects/disciplines

6. Proverbs 15:1 says that a peaceful heart turns away wrath.
   True
   False

7. Proverbs 9:10 says, "The fear of the Lord is the beginning of _____."
   a. knowledge
   b. wisdom
   c. understanding
   d. faith

● ECCLESIASTES

1. Most scholars believe that _____ authored Ecclesiastes.
   a. David
   b. Solomon
   c. Samuel
   d. Isaiah

2. Ecclesiastes 3:4 says that there is a time to weep and a time to laugh, a time to mourn and a time to sing.
   True
   False

3. Ecclesiastes 3:1 says that to everything there is a _____ and a time to every purpose under heaven.
   a. reason
   b. season
   c. truth
   d. mission

4. Ecclesiastes 4:9 says that two are better than one because they have a good return for their labor.
   True
   False

5. Ecclesiastes is one of the so-called wisdom books of the Old Testament.

   True

   False

⦿ SONG OF SOLOMON

1. Some Bible scholars believe Song of Solomon is a love
    song between King Solomon and _____.
    a. his wife
    b. a peasant girl tending his vineyards
    c. his first love
    d. a lost love

2. The lady compared the eyes of her lover to a deer's eyes.
    True
    False

3. According to Song of Solomon, love cannot be
    extinguished by _____.
    a. gossip
    b. boredom
    c. separation
    d. many waters

4. Solomon was crowned by his mother.
    True
    False

5. Song of Solomon is also known as the Song of Songs.
    True
    False

● ISAIAH

1. The book of Isaiah was written about seven hundred years before _____.
    a. the birth of Christ
    b. the destruction of Jerusalem
    c. the start of the early church
    d. the great flood

2. Beginning with the words "Unto us a child is born, unto us a son is given," Isaiah 9:6–7 is one of the most famous Old Testament prophecies about the coming messiah. Which of the following is not one of the titles that the verses give to the son?
    a. Wonderful Counselor
    b. Everlasting Father
    c. King of Kings
    d. Prince of Peace

3. Hezekiah, the king of Judah, was on his deathbed when God granted him fifteen additional years to live.
    True
    False

4. Isaiah 53 prophesies about the coming messiah's
    _____.

    a. earthly life
    b. sacrifice for mankind's sins
    c. A and B
    d. None of the above

5. Isaiah calls God _____ in Isaiah 12:2.
    a. Jehovah
    b. Jaireh
    c. The Great I Am
    d. Messiah

6. Isaiah never got the chance to see God in person.
    True
    False

7. Isaiah 11:6 states that the wolf will dwell with the
    _____ in a time of peace after the end times.

    a. lion
    b. lamb
    c. leopard
    d. tiger

● JEREMIAH

1. Jeremiah's name means _____.
   a. repent
   b. may Jehovah exalt
   c. child of God
   d. the Lord leads

2. Jeremiah is known as the prophet of hope.
   True
   False

3. Where was Jeremiah from?
   a. Jerusalem
   b. Anathoth
   c. Galilee
   d. Bethlehem

4. God made a covenant with Israel that he would forgive his people if they obeyed his law.
   True
   False

5. According to Jeremiah, _____ was worse than Israel in its unfaithfulness to the Lord.
   a. Babylon
   b. Syria
   c. Judah
   d. Assyria

6. God commanded Jeremiah not to get married.
   True
   False

7. God threatened to turn Jerusalem into a den of _____.
   a. dragons
   b. thieves
   c. lions
   d. doom

8. While calling Jeremiah to be his prophet, God showed Jeremiah the rod of a fig tree.
   True
   False

⬤ LAMENTATIONS

1. Evidence strongly suggests that _____ authored Lamentations.
    a. Isaiah
    b. Solomon
    c. David
    d. Jeremiah

2. Lamentations is a lament for _____.
    a. Judah's shameless idolatry and Babylon's destruction of Jerusalem
    b. how foreign nations raided Israel
    c. the absence of angels to protect Judah and Jerusalem
    d. All of the above

3. Lamentations is a _____.
    a. gathering of faith-filled stories
    b. collection of five poems
    c. diary of a despondent prophet
    d. chronology of Old Testament events

4. Jerusalem was called the daughter of Zion.
   True
   False

5. Zion is another name for _____.
    a. Judah
    b. Middle East
    c. Israel
    d. Philistine

6. After Jerusalem's destruction, basic necessities were so hard to come by that the Israelites had to purchase _____ from others.
    a. water and oil
    b. water and wood
    c. oil and wood
    d. milk and water

7. The Lord destroyed Jerusalem, including the palaces and altars.
    True
    False

● EZEKIEL

1. Who was Ezekiel?
    a. shepherd
    b. priest
    c. wise man
    d. astronomer

2. Ezekiel's mission from God was to _____.
    a. warn Israel that foreign nations were about to attack
    b. point the Israelites to the coming messiah
    c. proclaim God's word to the Israelites in Babylon
    d. bring peace to the Middle East

3. Who gave Ezekiel a scroll to eat?
    a. an angel
    b. the Lord
    c. Ezekiel's father
    d. Elijah

4. The scroll tasted like _____.
    a. honey
    b. barley
    c. manna
    d. cardboard

5. Ezekiel saw dry bones raised to life that looked to him like a large army.

   True

   False

6. Who was Ezekiel's father?

   a. Buzi

   b. Uz

   c. Uzziah

   d. Methuselah

7. Ezekiel is considered one of the Bible's minor prophets.

   True

   False

● DANIEL

1. Daniel was the last of the _____.
   a. Israelite kings
   b. major prophets
   c. sons of David
   d. Mohicans

2. Daniel interpreted what king's dream?
   a. Darius
   b. Nebuchadnezzar
   c. Saul
   d. Josiah

3. Which of the following men refused to bow down to a golden idol in Daniel 3:16–18?
   a. Shadrach
   b. Abednego
   c. Meshach
   d. All of the above

4. The Babylonian chief official changed Daniel's name to

   _____.
   a. Jehoshaphat
   b. Belteshazzar
   c. Meshach
   d. Belshazzar

5. Where was Daniel sent to for praying to God and not the king?
    a. lions' den
    b. prison
    c. exile
    d. Patmos

6. Who protected Shadrach, Meshach, and Abednego in the fiery furnace?
    a. the angel Gabriel
    b. the hand of God
    c. Elijah
    d. the son of God

7. What did King Nebuchadnezzar say when he saw Shadrach, Meshach, and Abednego safe in the fiery furnace?
    a. "Make the furnace seven times hotter."
    b. "Forgive me, Lord, for I have sinned."
    c. "Blessed be the God of Shadrach, Meshach, and Abednego."
    d. "Glory to God in the highest."

8. God judged Nebuchadnezzar's pride by making him insane like an animal for seven years.
    True
    False

9. Daniel, Shadrach, Meshach, and Abednego drank water instead of the king's wine in order to remain pure and devoted to God.

   True

   False

10. Daniel dreamed of four _____ rising out of the sea, representing four kingdoms that would eventually succumb to God's kingdom.

    a. serpents

    b. ships

    c. leviathan

    d. beasts

11. The angel Gabriel is Israel's great prince and protector.

    True

    False

● HOSEA

1. Which king did not rule over Judah during Hosea's four decades as a prophet?
   a. Jotham
   b. Uzziah
   c. Hezekiah
   d. Jehoshaphat

2. In the book of Hosea, those who walk in the ways of the Lord are _____.
   a. righteous
   b. faithful
   c. just
   d. pure

3. The Lord reminds Israel that its hope is in him.
   True
   False

4. Hosea 12:3 says that _____ grabbed his brother by the heel in their mother's womb.
   a. Esau
   b. Jacob
   c. Saul
   d. David

5. Hosea is the last of the books of the minor prophets.

   True

   False

JOEL

1. The Lord will gather all nations where?
   a. in the valley of Jehoshaphat
   b. in Jerusalem
   c. in Solomon's temple
   d. at the Mount of Olives

2. Joel 3:21 says the Lord will cleanse the blood of people throughout the earth.
   True
   False

3. Scholars generally believe that Joel lived in _____.
   a. Israel
   b. Judah
   c. Babylon
   d. Rome

4. In his book, Joel preaches to the people of Judah.
   True
   False

5. The name Joel means "The Lord is God."
   True
   False

● AMOS

1. Which is true of Amos?
    a. He was a scribe from Jerusalem.
    b. He was a shepherd from Tekoa.
    c. He was a fisherman from Engedi.
    d. He was a farmer from Dothan.

2. Who was king of Israel when Amos wrote the book bearing his name?
    a. Jeroboam
    b. Uzziah
    c. Darius
    d. Asa

3. The name Amos means "borne" or "a burden."
    True
    False

4. Amos was one of ten minor prophets.
    True
    False

5. Amos 1:2 says the Lord's voice sounds like a _____.
   a. whisper
   b. whirlwind
   c. roar
   d. trumpet

● OBADIAH

1. Obadiah prophesied against _____ for the sin of pride.
   a. Judah
   b. Babylon
   c. Edom
   d. Nineveh

2. Obadiah had a vision of Israel (the house of Joseph) as a flame.
   True
   False

3. Obadiah is the shortest book in the _____.
   a. Old Testament
   b. New Testament
   c. Bible
   d. A and C

4. Obadiah was one of the Bible's minor prophets.
   True
   False

5. The name Obadiah means "slave of Yahweh."
   True
   False

✹ JONAH

1. God told Jonah to go to _____ and warn the
   people to repent of their sinful ways.
   a. Nineveh
   b. Damascus
   c. Rome
   d. Jerusalem

2. Jonah hopped on a ship to what city to run away from God?
   a. Bethlehem
   b. Joppa
   c. Tarshish
   d. Jerusalem

3. How did the ship's crew calm the raging storm sent by
   God?
   a. prayed
   b. threw Jonah overboard
   c. cast lots
   d. cried out to God for mercy

4. How was Jonah rescued from drowning in the raging sea?
   a. A passing ship picked him up.
   b. Jonah walked on water.
   c. A great fish swallowed him.
   d. Jonah swam to a deserted island.

5. How long did Jonah stay in the belly of a great fish?
   a. 3 days
   b. 7 days
   c. 40 days and 40 nights
   d. overnight

6. Jonah warned the Ninevites that they had _____ days before the Lord would destroy their city if they didn't turn from their sin.
   a. 40
   b. 30
   c. 20
   d. 3 days and 3 nights

7. What was the Ninevites' response to Jonah's message?
   a. They ran Jonah out of town.
   b. They believed God and fasted.
   c. They rejected the message and continued in sin.
   d. They ignored the message, and the city was destroyed.

8. God supplied a tree to shade Jonah while he waited in the heat for Nineveh's destruction.
   True
   False

9. Nineveh was located in what country?
    a. Babylon
    b. Greece
    c. Assyria
    d. Syria

10. At the end of the book, Jonah argues with God about the plant he'd received and about what should happen to Nineveh.
    True
    False

● MICAH

1. Micah 5:2 prophesies that the coming messiah will be born in what city?
   a. Jerusalem
   b. Bethlehem
   c. Galilee
   d. Nazareth

2. The prophecy in Micah 5:2 is later quoted in Matthew 2:6.
   True
   False

3. In Micah 2:1, the Lord says woe to them who _____ and _____.
   a. plan iniquity; plot evil on their beds
   b. plan without prayer; plot evil on their beds
   c. plan iniquity; plot evil in their hearts
   d. plan without prayer; plot evil in their hearts

4. Micah 4:6 indicates that Micah was deeply concerned for those less fortunate in society.
   True
   False

5. Micah accurately predicts in Micah 1:6 that Israel would fall to the Assyrian Empire.

    True

    False

● NAHUM

1. Nahum is considered one of the major prophets of the Bible.
   True
   False

2. What are the clouds, according to Nahum 1:3?
   a. God's pillows
   b. the dust of God's feet
   c. gifts bestowed from heaven
   d. signs of the Lord's mercy and grace

3. To which city was Nahum a prophet?
   a. Rome
   b. Tarshish
   c. Joppa
   d. Nineveh

4. In Nahum 3:1, Nahum declares woe to the bloody city; it is full of perversion and iniquity.
   True
   False

5. Nahum's city had robbed and pillaged _____.
   a. Israel
   b. Judah
   c. all the neighboring countries
   d. Greece

● HABAKKUK

1. What does the name Habakkuk mean?
   a. to embrace
   b. to stand firm in the faith
   c. to wrestle
   d. A and C

2. God used which nation to bring judgment on Judah for its disobedience?
   a. Babylon
   b. Egypt
   c. Assyria
   d. Philistine

3. Habakkuk was considered one of the twelve minor prophets.
   True
   False

4. Habakkuk 2:4 says the just will live by his _____.
   a. grace
   b. faith
   c. mercy
   d. truth

5. Habakkuk was written around 620 BC.
   True
   False

● ZEPHANIAH

1. What does God do each morning, according to Zephaniah 3:5?
   a. bring his judgment to light
   b. strengthen his people
   c. breathe life into every living creature
   d. bestow us with mercy and grace

2. Zephaniah 2:3 implores readers to seek _____ in order to be sheltered on the day of the Lord's anger.
   a. glory and honor
   b. first the kingdom of God
   c. righteousness and humility
   d. God's protection and care

3. Zephaniah means "the Lord has concealed" or "the Lord has protected."
   True
   False

4. Zephaniah was a prophet during the reign of King _____.
   a. Uzziah
   b. Josiah
   c. Solomon
   d. Jeroboam

5. Zephaniah 1:1 traces Zephaniah's genealogy back four generations.
    True
    False

● HAGGAI

1. Haggai wrote this book to the Jews of Jerusalem in 520 BC, nearly twenty years after they returned from exile in Babylon.

    True

    False

2. The book of Haggai contains four messages for the people of Judah. What do these messages primarily convey?

    a. to finish rebuilding the temple
    b. to make God central in their lives to receive his future blessings
    c. A and B
    d. None of the above

3. After they returned from exile to their homeland, the Israelites experienced a drought. Why?

    a. They had forgotten how to farm.
    b. They didn't immediately rebuild the temple.
    c. They built altars to Baal.
    d. They groveled over the condition of the nation.

● ZECHARIAH

1. Zechariah 12:9 says the Lord will _____ any nation that comes against Jerusalem.
   a. block
   b. destroy
   c. turn away
   d. None of the above

2. Zechariah has an ongoing conversation with _____ throughout chapters 1 to 6 of his book.
   a. God
   b. David
   c. Jesus
   d. an angel

3. Zechariah 10:4 is a prophecy that Jesus would be the _____ of the Christian church.
   a. cornerstone
   b. rock
   c. founder
   d. savior

4. Zechariah was a prophet of Judah and the son of Berechiah.
   True
   False

5. The name Zechariah means "Yahweh remembers."
   True
   False

● MALACHI

1. The second chapter of Malachi is the last chapter of the Old Testament.
   True
   False

2. After Malachi, the prophetic voice was silent for the next _____, until the gospel accounts.
   a. 1,000 years
   b. 400 years
   c. 200 years
   d. 100 years

3. The final chapter of Malachi says that God will send a prophet before the coming of the great day of Yahweh. Who is the prophet?
   a. Noah
   b. Moses
   c. Elijah
   d. Abraham

4. The first few verses of Malachi remind Israelites that _____.
   a. God is faithful
   b. God is good
   c. God rewards obedience
   d. God loves them

5. Malachi is the last of the minor prophets.

True

False

Old Testament Answer Keys

GENESIS—ANSWERS

1. C (See Genesis 2:22)
2. D (See Genesis 1:1)
3. D (See Genesis 2:7)
4. False (God told them not to eat from this tree.)
5. C (See Genesis 3:1)
6. B (See Genesis 3:7)
7. C (See Genesis 3:24)
8. True (See Genesis 4:2)
9. A (See Genesis 4:3–4)
10. D (See Genesis 4:7)
11. D (See Genesis 5:27)
12. B (See Genesis 5:32)
13. A (See Genesis 6:5, 11–13)
14. D (See Genesis 7:17)
15. D (See Genesis 7:6)
16. C (See Genesis 9:13)
17. A (See Genesis 11:2)

18. A (See Genesis 11:7–9)

19. B (See Genesis 12:1–2)

20. C (See Genesis 21:5)

21. A (See Genesis 21:3)

22. D (See Genesis 25:29–34)

23. B (See Genesis 35:22–26)

24. False (Potiphar's wife accused him of rape.)

25. B (See Genesis 41:41–46)

26. False (to buy grain; see Genesis 42:3)

27. B (See Genesis 44:1–12)

28. True (See Genesis 14:18)

29. True (See Genesis 19:24)

30. False (a pillar of salt; see Genesis 19:26)

EXODUS—ANSWERS

1. C (See Exodus 5:7)

2. A (See Exodus 5:10–11)

3. A (See Exodus 3:1–4)

4. B (See Exodus 20:1–17)

5. D (See Exodus 4:18–31)

6. C

7. B (See Exodus 14:20–22)

8. False (Aaron threw down the staff; see Exodus 7:8–13)

9. A (See Exodus 2:21)

10. D (See Exodus 31:18)

11. B (See Exodus 6:20)

12. False (Moses was 80; see Exodus 7:7)

13. C (See Exodus 12:40)

14. True (See Exodus 7:17)

15. True (See Exodus 10:22)

16. A (See Exodus 11:5)

17. D (See Exodus 14:7)

18. True (See Exodus 12)

19. False (The stones represented the twelve sons of Israel; see Exodus 28:21)

20. B (See Exodus 26:31)

LEVITICUS—ANSWERS

1. B

2. C (See Leviticus 19:9–10)

3. C (See Leviticus 10:1–2)

4. True (See Leviticus 4)

5. True (See Leviticus 9)

NUMBERS—ANSWERS

1. A (See Numbers 9:15–16)

2. A (See Numbers 9:17)

3. B (See Numbers 20:11)

4. C (See Numbers 20:12)

5. A (See Numbers 1:3)

6. False (the tribe of Levi; see Numbers 3:6)

DEUTERONOMY—ANSWERS

1. D (See Deuteronomy 5:7)
2. B (See Deuteronomy 5:12)
3. False (The sixth commandment is thou shalt not murder.)
4. A (See Deuteronomy 5:20)
5. True (See Deuteronomy 5:21)
6. D (See Deuteronomy 6:3)
7. False (Moses saw it from a distance; see Deuteronomy 3:27)
8. C (See Deuteronomy 5:16)
9. A
10. C

JOSHUA—ANSWERS

1. C (See Joshua 1:1–9)
2. A (See Joshua 2:1)
3. True (See Joshua 2:4–7)
4. B (See Joshua 6:3–4)
5. D (See Joshua 3:15–16)
6. False (seven days; see Joshua 6:2)

JUDGES—ANSWERS

1. A (See Judges 10:4–5)
2. B (See Judges 3:9)
3. D (See Judges 7:1–8)
4. C (See Judges 16:19)
5. B (See Judges 4 and 5)

6. False (300 foxes; see Judges 15)
7. False (if the fleece was wet but the ground was dry; see Judges 6:37)

RUTH—ANSWERS

1. A (See Ruth 1:1)
2. B (See Ruth 4:13–21)
3. False (Ruth said this.)
4. True (See Ruth 1:2)
5. True (See Ruth 4:10–13)

1 AND 2 SAMUEL—ANSWERS

1. B (See 1 Samuel 16:18)
2. A (See 1 Samuel 1:18–20)
3. C (See 1 Samuel 8:2)
4. B (See 1 Samuel 15:23)
5. D (See 1 Samuel 31:4)
6. False (sling and one stone)
7. C
8. A (See 1 Samuel 16:1–13)
9. B (See 2 Samuel 4:5)
10. True (See 2 Samuel 11:1–27)

1 AND 2 KINGS—ANSWERS

1. C (See 2 Kings 5:1, 14)
2. C (See 1 Kings 3:26–27)

3. True (See 2 Kings 2:11)

4. B (See 2 Kings 22:1)

5. A

1 AND 2 CHRONICLES—ANSWERS

1. D (See 2 Chronicles 23:1, 11)

2. A (See 2 Chronicles 36:21)

3. True (See 1 Chronicles 3:9)

4. B (See 1 Chronicles 22:6)

5. False (He even consulted a medium; see 1 Chronicles 10:13)

6. C (See 2 Chronicles 1:10)

7. True (See 2 Chronicles 8:1)

8. False (forty years; see 2 Chronicles 9:30)

EZRA—ANSWERS

1. C (See Ezra 4:21)

2. A (See Ezra 5:1–2)

3. False (Darius reigned after Cyrus; see Ezra 4:5)

4. True

5. True

NEHEMIAH—ANSWERS

1. B (See Nehemiah 1:11)

2. D (See Nehemiah 2:1)

3. A (See Nehemiah 1–3)

4. True (See Nehemiah 4:16)

5. True (See Nehemiah 10:1)

ESTHER—ANSWERS

1. C (See Esther 1:9)
2. C
3. A (See Esther 1:1)
4. B (See Esther 2:17)
5. False (She was Mordecai's cousin; see Esther 2:7)
6. D (See Esther 2:7)
7. B (See Esther 7)

JOB—ANSWERS

1. False (Satan could not harm Job physically; see Job 1:12)
2. B (See Job 1:18–19)
3. C (See Job 40:6)
4. D (See Job 1:21–22)
5. D (See Job 23:12)
6. False (It was Eliphaz, Bildad, and Zophar; see Job 2:11)
7. True (See Job 1:1)

PSALMS—ANSWERS

1. A
2. B
3. True
4. C
5. B
6. True
7. B (See Psalm 19:1)
8. True

9. D (See Psalm 25:7)
10. True

PROVERBS—ANSWERS

1. True
2. C
3. False (Trust in the Lord with all your heart, and do not lean on your own understanding.)
4. True
5. D
6. False (A soft answer turns away wrath; see Proverbs 15:1)
7. B

ECCLESIASTES—ANSWERS

1. B
2. False (a time to mourn and a time to dance)
3. B
4. True
5. True

SONG OF SOLOMON—ANSWERS

1. B
2. False (dove's eyes; see Song of Solomon 1:15)
3. D (See Song of Solomon 8:7)
4. True (See Song of Solomon 3:11)
5. True

ISAIAH—ANSWERS

1. A
2. C
3. True (See Isaiah 38:1–5)
4. C
5. A
6. False (Isaiah saw the Lord in the year that King Uzziah died; see Isaiah 6:1)
7. B (See Isaiah 11:6)

JEREMIAH—ANSWERS

1. B
2. True
3. B (See Jeremiah 1:1)
4. False
5. C (See Jeremiah 3:11)
6. True (See Jeremiah 16:2)
7. A (See Jeremiah 9:11)
8. False (God shows him an almond branch; see Jeremiah 1:11)

LAMENTATIONS—ANSWERS

1. D
2. A
3. B
4. True (See Lamentations 1:6)
5. C

6. B (See Lamentations 5:4)

7. True (See Lamentations 2:7)

EZEKIEL—ANSWERS

1. B (See Ezekiel 1:3)

2. C (See Ezekiel 2:3)

3. B (See Ezekiel 3:2–3)

4. A (See Ezekiel 3:3)

5. True (See Ezekiel 37:10)

6. A (See Ezekiel 1:3)

7. False (He is a major prophet.)

DANIEL—ANSWERS

1. B

2. B (See Daniel 2:24)

3. D

4. B (See Daniel 1:7)

5. A (See Daniel 6:22)

6. D (See Daniel 3:25)

7. C (See Daniel 3:28)

8. True (See Daniel 4)

9. True (See Daniel 1:12)

10. D (See Daniel 7:3)

11. False (Michael; see Daniel 12:1)

HOSEA—ANSWERS

1. D (See Hosea 1:1)
2. C (See Hosea 14:9)
3. True (See Hosea 13:9)
4. B
5. False (It's the first.)

JOEL—ANSWERS

1. A (See Joel 3:1–2)
2. False (He will avenge the blood of his chosen people Israel.)
3. B
4. True
5. True

AMOS—ANSWERS

1. B (See Amos 1:1)
2. A (See Amos 1:1)
3. True
4. False (12)
5. C

OBADIAH—ANSWERS

1. C (See Obadiah 1:10–14)
2. True (See Obadiah 1:18)
3. A
4. True
5. False (worshipper of Yahweh)

JONAH—ANSWERS

1. A (See Jonah 3:4)
2. C (See Jonah 1:3)
3. B (See Jonah 1:15)
4. C (See Jonah 1:17)
5. A (See Jonah 1:17)
6. A (See Jonah 3:4)
7. B (See Jonah 3:5)
8. False (vine; see Jonah 4:6)
9. C (See Jonah 1:2)
10. True (See Jonah 4:1)

MICAH—ANSWERS

1. B
2. True
3. A
4. True
5. True

NAHUM—ANSWERS

1. False (minor prophet)
2. B
3. D (See Nahum 1:11)
4. False (full of lies and plunder)
5. C

HABAKKUK—ANSWERS

1. D
2. A (See Habakkuk 1:6)
3. True
4. B
5. True

ZEPHANIAH—ANSWERS

1. A
2. C
3. True
4. B
5. True

HAGGAI—ANSWERS

1. True
2. C
3. B (See Haggai 1)

ZECHARIAH—ANSWERS

1. B
2. D
3. A
4. True (See Zechariah 1:1)
5. True

MALACHI—ANSWERS

1. False (Malachi has four chapters.)
2. B
3. C
4. D (See Malachi 1:1–5)
5. True

New Testament Questions

● MATTHEW

1. Quoting the prophet Isaiah, Matthew tells us that one name for Jesus will be Immanuel, which means

   _____.

   a. God reigns
   b. God saves
   c. God with us
   d. God for us

2. Which of the following were not one of the three things that the devil tempted Jesus to do before Jesus began his public ministry?
   a. turn stones to bread
   b. jump off a building
   c. worship the devil
   d. walk on water

3. According to Jesus, the wise man builds his house on
   _____, while the fool builds his house on _____.
   a. rock; sand
   b. foundation; swamp
   c. his word; falsehood
   d. God; Satan

4. Complete the verse: "Come to me, all who labor and are
   heavy laden, and I will give you _____."
   a. peace
   b. rest
   c. strength
   d. life to the full

5. Complete the verse: "For my _____ is easy, and my
   _____ is light."
   a. burden; yoke
   b. way; mission
   c. yoke; burden
   d. way; burden

6. Jesus says the kingdom of heaven is like _____.
   a. a mustard seed
   b. an olive tree
   c. a wonderful party
   d. a camel's eye

7. The traditional names of the three magi, or wise men, who visited the baby Jesus are Balthazar, Melchior, and Caspar.

   True

   False

8. Which magi is said to have given the gift of frankincense?
   a. Melchior
   b. Balthazar
   c. Joash
   d. Jeroboam

9. What was the name of Jesus's stepfather?
   a. Nicodemus
   b. Simon
   c. Caiaphas
   d. Joseph

10. Mary and Joseph were married when Jesus was born.

    True

    False

11. What was Matthew's occupation prior to becoming a disciple?
    a. fisherman
    b. shepherd
    c. innkeeper
    d. tax collector

12. Mary and Joseph fled from King Herod to _____.
    a. Jerusalem
    b. Galilee
    c. Egypt
    d. Babylon

13. Who told Mary and Joseph to take Jesus and flee for
    another country when Jesus was a young boy?
    a. Herod
    b. the magi
    c. John the Baptist
    d. an angel of the Lord

14. After Jesus was baptized, God's Spirit descended from
    heaven in the form of an eagle.
    True
    False

15. Jesus was baptized by _____.
    a. John the Baptist
    b. Joseph
    c. Nicodemus
    d. the Sanhedrin

16. How did King Herod kill John the Baptist?
    a. crucifixion
    b. lions' den
    c. fiery furnace
    d. beheading

17. How many men did Jesus feed using just five loaves of bread and two fish?
    a. 4,000
    b. 5,000
    c. 6,000
    d. 7,000

18. How long did Jesus fast in the desert?
    a. 7 days
    b. 30 days
    c. 40 days
    d. 60 days

19. Who betrayed Jesus and got him arrested?
    a. Judas
    b. Caiaphas
    c. Peter
    d. Thomas

20. Jesus was betrayed for _____.
    a. a kiss
    b. 30 pieces of silver
    c. political power
    d. revenge

21. When Jesus was arrested, one of his disciples reacted by cutting off an ear of the high priest's slave with a sword.
    True
    False

22. How many times did Peter deny knowing Jesus when someone identified him as a disciple in the courtyard?
    a. once
    b. twice
    c. three times
    d. four times

23. From the sixth hour to the ninth hour, as Jesus hung on the cross, there was _____ over all the land.
    a. darkness
    b. a thunderstorm
    c. mourning
    d. an earthquake

24. After Jesus died, the temple walls split in two from top to bottom.

    True

    False

25. After witnessing the earth quake and rocks split and other miraculous events following Jesus's death, the Roman centurion and others guarding Jesus said, _____
    a. "Truly this was the king of the Jews."
    b. "Truly this was the Son of God."
    c. "Truly we are under God's judgment."
    d. "Truly this man was a prophet of God."

26. _____ committed suicide before Jesus's resurrection.
    a. Caiaphas
    b. Bartholomew
    c. Peter
    d. Judas

27. Tax collectors like Matthew were among the most popular people in Jewish society.

    True

    False

28. Jesus told Peter to forgive someone _____.
    a. 70 × 7 times (490 times)
    b. 70 times
    c. 7 times
    d. 325 times

29. Jesus said the two greatest commandments are to love
    God with all your heart, soul, mind, and strength and to
    love your neighbor as yourself.
    True
    False

● MARK

1. Where was Jesus baptized?
   a. Nile River
   b. Jordan River
   c. Sea of Galilee
   d. Sistine Chapel

2. After Jesus was baptized, God spoke from the heavens, "This is my beloved Son, in whom I am well pleased."
   True
   False

3. The disciples John and _____ were brothers.
   a. Peter
   b. Andrew
   c. Matthew
   d. James

4. Jesus was _____ as the disciples took a boat across a lake.
   a. praying
   b. teaching
   c. sleeping
   d. walking on water

5. What did Jesus do when the raging storm shook the boat and frightened the disciples?
   a. rebuked and calmed the storm
   b. prayed for wisdom
   c. walked on water
   d. rebuked the disciples' lack of faith

6. Jesus revived Jairus's dead daughter after she had been in a tomb for three days.
   True
   False

7. Jesus healed a deaf man with a speech impediment by
   _____.
   a. putting mud on his ears
   b. inserting his fingers into his ears
   c. laying hands on him
   d. shouting at him

8. Who believed that Jesus was John the Baptist?
   a. Caiaphas
   b. Pilate
   c. Herod
   d. Nicodemus

9. John the Baptist was Jesus's uncle.
   True
   False

10. The first two disciples that Jesus called were

    _____.

    a. James and John
    b. Thomas and Bartholomew
    c. Matthew and Judas
    d. Peter and Andrew

11. John the Baptist lived in the wilderness, eating _____
    and wild honey.
    a. wild boar
    b. locusts
    c. wild berries
    d. beetles

12. James and John were the sons of _____.
    a. Zebedee
    b. Zechariah
    c. Zacchaeus
    d. Zephaniah

13. Four men brought a paralyzed man on a mat for Jesus to heal in Capernaum. When they couldn't carry the man inside the door of the home where Jesus was teaching, what did they do?
    a. healed him themselves
    b. touched Jesus's cloak
    c. cut a hole in the roof and lowered the man inside
    d. prayed for a miracle and saw Jesus come outside

14. Jesus said the Sabbath was made for _____.
    a. God's glory
    b. man
    c. rest
    d. worship

15. Which of the following was not one of Jesus's twelve disciples?
    a. Bartholomew
    b. Thaddaeus
    c. Matthias
    d. Philip

16. The teachers of the law accused Jesus of being possessed by Beelzebub.
    True
    False

17. Jesus said the kingdom of God is like a _____.
    a. vine and branches
    b. house built on a rock
    c. little child
    d. mustard seed

18. What was the name given for the demons that Jesus drove out of a possessed man and into a herd of pigs?
    a. Legion
    b. Beelzebub
    c. Baal
    d. None of the above

19. Jesus said a prophet is not without honor except in

    _____.

    a. Hades
    b. his own town
    c. spiritual darkness
    d. his own family

20. After Jesus fed thousands of people, the disciples picked up _____ basketfuls of leftover bread and fish.
    a. 5
    b. 7
    c. 12
    d. 40

21. When the disciples saw Jesus walking on the lake, they thought he was an apparition.

    True

    False

22. What did Jesus do to heal the blind man at Bethsaida?

    a. spit on his eyes and put his hands on them
    b. poured water over his eyes
    c. A and B
    d. None of the above

23. What did Peter say Jesus was in Mark 8:29?

    a. King of the Jews
    b. the promised Savior
    c. Lord of lords
    d. the Messiah

24. Who appeared before Jesus, Peter, James, and John at the transfiguration?

    a. Abraham
    b. Elijah
    c. Moses
    d. B and C

25. Jesus said the kingdom of God belongs to little children.

    True

    False

26. On which present-day holiday did Jesus ride triumphantly on a donkey into Jerusalem to adoring crowds?
    a. Easter
    b. Good Friday
    c. Palm Sunday
    d. Maundy Thursday

27. Though he doesn't identify himself in the book, who is generally considered the author of Mark?
    a. John Mark
    b. Matthew
    c. Luke
    d. John

28. Jeremiah is the first prophet quoted in Mark.
    True
    False

29. Mark was _____.
    a. a shepherd
    b. an evangelist
    c. a fisherman
    d. a chief priest

30. Jesus told believers who wanted to come after him to deny themselves, take up their _____, and follow him.
    a. cross
    b. burdens
    c. prayers
    d. inmost being

31. How did the women react after seeing Jesus's tomb empty and hearing from a mysterious man in a white robe that Jesus had risen?
    a. They were perplexed.
    b. They were despondent.
    c. They were afraid.
    d. They celebrated.

● LUKE

1. Luke's first chapter has eighty verses. How many verses include women speaking?
   a. 3
   b. 18
   c. 29
   d. 50

2. What is the name of the angel who announced to Mary that she would conceive the "Son of the Most High"?
   a. Michael
   b. David
   c. Raphael
   d. Gabriel

3. The first thing Mary says in Luke's gospel is in reaction to the angel's announcement that she would conceive God's Son: "How will this be, since I am a virgin?"
   True
   False

4. Complete this verse, the first line of the song that Mary sings after the angel reveals that she will conceive a baby by the Holy Spirit: "My soul _____ the Lord, and my spirit rejoices in God my savior."

   a. loves

   b. exalts

   c. magnifies

   d. praises

5. What are the names of the two righteous people who celebrate the presentation of the baby Jesus?

   a. Simeon and Anna

   b. Phanuel and Elizabeth

   c. Simon and Ananias

   d. Zacchaeus and Sapphira

6. Complete the verse: "And Jesus increased in _____ and in _____ and in favor with God and man."

   a. wisdom; understanding

   b. manhood; authority

   c. understanding; grace

   d. wisdom; stature

7. As John the Baptist prepared the way for Jesus, how did he describe himself?
   a. a snake in the grass
   b. a flame in the desert
   c. a voice in the wilderness
   d. a locust in camel hair

8. John the Baptist considered himself unworthy to do what to Jesus?
   a. baptize him
   b. kiss his feet
   c. untie his sandal
   d. be baptized by him

9. At the beginning of his ministry, Jesus came to Nazareth and entered the synagogue. From which scroll did he read?
   a. Exodus
   b. Isaiah
   c. Psalms
   d. Jeremiah

10. Complete this quote, which the demon-possessed man from Capernaum said to Jesus: "What have you to do with us, Jesus of Nazareth? Have you come to destroy us? I know who you are—the _____ of God."
    a. Holy One
    b. Christ
    c. Son
    d. Angel

11. Which of the following disciples was convinced to follow Jesus because of the massive number of fish that Jesus caused him to catch?
    a. Andrew
    b. Matthew
    c. Simon the Zealot
    d. Simon Peter

12. What afflicted the man whose friends lowered him into a house in order to get him healed by Jesus?
    a. blindness
    b. leprosy
    c. paralysis
    d. gout

13. Which of these occupations does Jesus use as a metaphor for his own work in the world?

    a. surgeon

    b. physician

    c. midwife

    d. masseuse

14. According to Luke's gospel, which of these disciples' names is not shared by another apostle? That is, all of the following disciples' names could represent two disciples, except one—which is it?

    a. John

    b. Simon

    c. Judas

    d. James

15. Complete this verse spoken by Jesus to his disciples: "But love _____, and do good, and lend, expecting nothing in return, and your reward will be great, and you will be sons of the Most High, for He is kind to the ungrateful and the evil."

    a. the body of Christ

    b. your enemies

    c. one another

    d. your neighbor as yourself

16. Luke dedicated his book to Theophilus.

    True

    False

17. Who were the first people to learn the news of Jesus's birth?

    a.   high priests

    b.   Caesar Augustus's court

    c.   shepherds

    d.   None of the above

18. When the shepherds visited Jesus, he was in a _____.

    a.   home

    b.   stable

    c.   palace

    d.   temple

19. The shepherds found Jesus wrapped in _____.

    a.   a manger

    b.   donkey saddle blankets

    c.   camel hair

    d.   swaddling clothes

20. Jesus did not get circumcised because he was the Son of God.

    True

    False

21. Jesus's hometown was _____.
    a. Nazareth
    b. Galilee
    c. Bethlehem
    d. Capernaum

22. Jesus began his public ministry at about age _____.
    a. 18
    b. 21
    c. 30
    d. 33

23. Jesus's genealogy traces back to _____.
    a. David
    b. Jacob
    c. Adam
    d. All of the above

24. Jesus told the leper he healed to tell all his friends about the miracle.
    True
    False

25. "Blessed are you who weep now, for you shall laugh" is one of the _____ that Jesus taught.
    a. Sermons on the Mount
    b. Beatitudes
    c. Parables
    d. Homilies

26. Which of the following women did Jesus not heal of evil spirits and infirmities?
    a. Mary Magdalene
    b. Martha
    c. Joanna
    d. Susanna

27. The parable of the Good Samaritan taught a lesson on how to treat your _____.
    a. family
    b. work associates
    c. neighbor
    d. spouse

28. Jesus said, "My mother and my brothers are those who hear the word of God and do it."
    True
    False

29. On the Sabbath, Jesus healed a man suffering from _____.

    a. leprosy

    b. demonic possession

    c. blindness

    d. dropsy

30. Of the ten lepers Jesus healed, how many returned to thank him?

    a. 10

    b. 1

    c. 5

    d. 9

⊛ JOHN

1. According to John, Jesus Christ, the Word of God, is full of grace and _____.
   a. mercy
   b. power
   c. truth
   d. sacrifice

2. Jesus asked the woman at the well to give him _____.
   a. bread
   b. water
   c. faith
   d. a denarius

3. What significant event in Jesus's life happened by the brook Kidron?
   a. the transfiguration
   b. his arrest
   c. the Sermon on the Mount
   d. the Crucifixion

4. When John the Baptist saw Jesus, he said, "Behold,
   _____, who takes away the sin of the world!"
   a. the Son of God
   b. the Son of Man
   c. the Lamb of God
   d. the Messiah

5. Cephas is another name for Peter.
   True
   False

6. Jesus's first miracle recorded in John was _____.
   a. turning water into wine at a wedding
   b. healing a blind man
   c. walking on water
   d. driving out demons

7. Jesus told Nicodemus that no one could see the kingdom
   of God unless they were _____.
   a. following him
   b. devoted to God
   c. perfect
   d. born again

8. Nicodemus was a _____.
   a. Pharisee
   b. member of the Jewish ruling council
   c. prophet
   d. A and B

9. The Samaritan woman at the well offered Jesus living water.
   True
   False

10. The lame man whom Jesus healed at the pool of Bethsaida had been an invalid for _____.
    a. 20 years
    b. 30 years
    c. 35 years
    d. 38 years

11. Who provided the five small barley loaves and two fish that Jesus turned into food for thousands of men and their women and children?
    a. Andrew
    b. Peter
    c. a boy
    d. a local fish market

12. Jesus said he is the bread of life. Whoever comes to him will never go hungry.

    True

    False

13. What did Jesus tell the woman caught in adultery?
    a. "Go and sin no more."
    b. "Let anyone who is without sin cast the first stone."
    c. "Your sins are forgiven."
    d. "You must be born again."

14. Which of the following did Jesus not do to heal the blind man?
    a. told him to wash in the pool of Siloam
    b. spit in the man's eyes
    c. made mud with his saliva
    d. put the mud on the blind man's eyes

15. Which of the following titles did Jesus not give to himself?
    a. the gate for the sheep
    b. the good shepherd
    c. the chief of chiefs
    d. I am

16. How long was Lazarus in a tomb when Jesus raised him from the dead?
    a. 4 days
    b. 3 days
    c. 2 days
    d. 1 week

17. Caiaphas, the high priest, led the plot to kill Jesus.
    True
    False

18. A great crowd greeted Jesus as he rode a _____ into Jerusalem, fulfilling a prophecy in Zechariah 9:9.
    a. chariot
    b. horse
    c. donkey
    d. None of the above

19. Jesus said he is the _____.
    a. truth
    b. way
    c. life
    d. All of the above

20. Jesus washed all of the disciples' feet except for Judas's.
    True
    False

21. At the last supper, Jesus told Peter that _____ he
    would deny Jesus _____.
    a. before Jesus died; four times
    b. before the rooster crows; three times
    c. before Jesus died; three times
    d. before the rooster crows; four times

22. Jesus told the disciples the heavenly Father would send
    them _____ to help them and be with them forever.
    a. the Holy Spirit
    b. an advocate
    c. the Spirit of truth
    d. All of the above

23. On the night he was betrayed, Jesus prayed _____.
    a. for all believers
    b. for his disciples
    c. to be glorified
    d. All of the above

24. Jesus said he is the true vine and his Father is the
    vinedresser.
    True
    False

25. Where was Jesus arrested?
    a. the upper room
    b. a garden
    c. the temple
    d. a courtyard

26. Who handed Jesus to the Jewish officials to be crucified?
    a. Pilate
    b. Annas
    c. Caiaphas
    d. Herod

27. Jesus was crucified at the Place of the Skull, which in Aramaic is called Golgotha.
    True
    False

28. Pilate had a notice prepared and fastened to the cross. It read: Jesus of Nazareth, _____.
    a. Lord of lords
    b. a common criminal
    c. the King of the Jews
    d. the Savior of the world

29. Who was the only disciple who saw Jesus's crucifixion, according to the book of John?
    a. Peter
    b. James
    c. Matthew
    d. John

30. What were Jesus's final words before dying?
    a. "My God, my God, why have you forsaken me?"
    b. "It is finished."
    c. "Father, forgive them, for they do not know what they are doing."
    d. "Into your hands I commit my spirit."

31. Who divided Jesus's clothes among them and cast lots for his garment in fulfillment of the prophecy found in Psalm 18:22?
    a. Jewish officials
    b. chief priests
    c. Roman soldiers at Golgotha
    d. Barabbas and his henchmen

32. Who asked Pilate for Jesus's body after he died?
    a. Joseph of Arimathea
    b. Nicodemus
    c. Mary
    d. John

33. Mary Magdalene was the first person to notice that Jesus's tomb was empty on the third day after Jesus's crucifixion.

    True

    False

34. Which two disciples saw Jesus's empty tomb?
    a. Peter and John
    b. James and John
    c. Andrew and John
    d. Peter and Andrew

35. Mary, Jesus's mother, was the first person to see Jesus after his resurrection.

    True

    False

36. Jesus then appeared to his disciples, showing them his

    _____.

    a. grace
    b. forgiveness
    c. resurrected body
    d. hands and side

37. Which disciple was not around when Jesus first appeared to them?
    a. Peter
    b. Thomas
    c. Philip
    d. Bartholomew

38. Jesus told Thomas to touch his hands and his side in order to stop doubting and believe.
    True
    False

39. Thomas reacted to touching Jesus's side and hands by saying, _____
    a. "You're alive!"
    b. "You are my Savior!"
    c. "My Lord and my God!"
    d. "Glory to God in the highest!"

40. Which of the following explains why Jesus's signs and wonders were recorded in the book of John?
    a. that you may believe that Jesus is the Messiah
    b. that you may believe that Jesus is the Son of God
    c. that by believing you may have life in his name
    d. All of the above

● ACTS

1. On what modern holiday did the Holy Spirit come
    upon the disciples?
    a. Pentecost
    b. Passover
    c. Feast of Booths
    d. Christmas

2. What were the professions of Aquila and Priscilla?
    a. silversmiths
    b. linen traders
    c. sellers of purple goods
    d. tentmakers

3. Berea is where Jews and some Greek women responded
    favorably to the gospel proclaimed by Paul and Silas and
    "received the word with all eagerness, examining the
    Scriptures daily to see if these things were so."
    True
    False

4. Which of the following did Jesus not mention as locations where the disciples would be his witnesses?

    a. the ends of the earth

    b. Jerusalem

    c. Judea and Samaria

    d. Rome

5. Saul was on the road to _____ when he saw a great light and the Lord spoke to him and temporarily blinded him.

    a. Jerusalem

    b. Damascus

    c. Ephesus

    d. Arabia

6. Who wrote the book of Acts?

    a. Paul

    b. Barnabas

    c. Luke

    d. Lazarus

7. The book of Acts was written specifically for Theophilus.

    True

    False

8. Who consented to Stephen's death by stoning?
    a. Judas
    b. Caiaphas
    c. Saul
    d. Pontius Pilate

9. How many people were saved after Peter preached the gospel to them?
    a. 120
    b. 3,000
    c. 25,000
    d. 5,000

10. Saul was from _____.
    a. Corinth
    b. Rome
    c. Jerusalem
    d. Tarsus

11. Who replaced Judas among the disciples?
    a. Paul
    b. Luke
    c. Barnabas
    d. Matthias

12. The disciples were able to speak in tongues and raise people from the dead after the Holy Spirit first came upon them.

    True

    False

13. Paul was living in _____ as the book of Acts ended.

    a. Rome

    b. Jerusalem

    c. Macedonia

    d. Spain

14. Who freed Peter from jail after he was arrested by Herod?

    a. John

    b. the Romans

    c. an angel

    d. Paul

15. When the high priest told Peter and the apostles they were prohibited from sharing the gospel, they hid themselves.

    True

    False

● ROMANS

1. Who authored Romans?
   a. Peter
   b. Paul
   c. John
   d. Ananias

2. Paul wrote that he was not ashamed of the gospel because it was the power of God for the salvation of every Israelite who believed.
   True
   False

3. Romans 3:23 says that all have sinned and come short of

   _____.
   a. God's perfect standards
   b. fulfilling God's plans
   c. earning entrance into heaven
   d. the glory of God

4. Romans 1:17 says that the just live by _____.
   a. God's word alone
   b. faith
   c. love
   d. their good deeds

5. Romans 5:8 teaches that God demonstrates his love for us in that, while we were still sinners, Christ _____.

    a. died for us

    b. was praying for us in heaven

    c. offered us eternal life

    d. came to earth as a baby

6. Romans 3:10 says there is none righteous, not one person.
    True
    False

7. Romans 6:23 says the wages of sin is _____, but the gift of God is _____ through Jesus Christ our Lord.

    a. trouble on earth; approval

    b. hell; eternal life

    c. death; salvation

    d. death; eternal life

8. Romans 12:1 tells us to offer our bodies as _____.

    a. temples of the Holy Spirit

    b. instruments of righteousness

    c. living sacrifices

    d. thin and fit

9. At the time that Paul wrote Romans, he had not yet visited Rome.

   True

   False

10. Chapters 4 and 5 of Romans cover two famous Old Testament men:
    a. Elijah and Elisha
    b. Adam and Abraham
    c. Solomon and David
    d. David and Saul

11. Romans 8:38–39 says _____ can separate us from God's love.
    a. sin
    b. death
    c. gluttony
    d. nothing

12. According to Romans, most authority is established by God.

    True

    False

13. Who is the father of many nations?

    a. Abraham

    b. Adam

    c. David

    d. Peter

14. Romans 7 talks about the struggle between Paul's desire to obey the Lord and his sinful nature.

    True

    False

15. Romans is considered _____.

    a. an epistle

    b. a history book

    c. a love letter

    d. an allegory

● 1 AND 2 CORINTHIANS

1. 1 Corinthians 13 is commonly known as the _____ chapter.
    a. faith
    b. love
    c. discipleship
    d. evangelism

2. According to 1 Corinthians 15:26, the last enemy to be destroyed is _____.
    a. the devil
    b. terrorism
    c. the anti-Christ
    d. death

3. The top three spiritual gifts are faith, hope, and love.
    True
    False

4. How many times did Paul get beaten with rods?
    a. 1
    b. 13
    c. 5
    d. 7

5. What type of giver does God love, according to
   2 Corinthians 8:7?
   a. wealthy
   b. faithful
   c. cheerful
   d. generous

● GALATIANS

1: In Galatians and other letters, Paul describes the relationship that believers have to God through Christ as one of _____.
   a. princes
   b. students
   c. heirs
   d. slaves

2. Galatians 3:23 tells Christians that whatever they do, they should do it with all their heart, as they are working for

   _____.
   a. the kingdom of God
   b. the Lord
   c. the gospel
   d. their church

3. According to Paul, all of God's laws can be summarized in one commandment: _____.
   a. Do to others as you would have them do to you
   b. Love the Lord your God with all your heart, soul, mind, and strength
   c. Love your neighbor as yourself
   d. God helps those who help themselves

4. We become children of God by faith in Jesus Christ.

   True

   False

5. Which of the following is not part of the fruit of the Spirit?

   a. joy

   b. patience

   c. goodness

   d. tolerance

● EPHESIANS

1. Who wrote Ephesians?
   a. Timothy
   b. Paul
   c. Barnabas
   d. Augustine

2. Ephesians 2:4 says God is rich in _____.
   a. every good thing
   b. love
   c. mercy
   d. kindness

3. How are people saved, according to Ephesians 2:8–9?
   a. by grace through faith
   b. by good works
   c. by a mix of grace and good works
   d. by a mix of faith and good works

4. Christ is derived from the Greek word Christos, meaning Appointed One.
   True
   False

5. Ephesians 5:25 says that husbands should love their wives
   _____.

    a. as they love themselves

    b. with an everlasting love

    c. to the degree that their wives love them

    d. as Christ loved the church

● PHILIPPIANS

1. Paul urges his readers to work out their salvation with fear and _____.
   a. steadfastness
   b. good intentions
   c. trembling
   d. joy

2. In Philippians 4:13, Paul says he can do all things through _____ who gives him strength.
   a. his inner resources
   b. Christ
   c. the Holy Spirit
   d. faith

3. Philippians 2:6–7 says Jesus took the form of a _____ when he left heaven and came to earth as a man.
   a. baby
   b. holy man
   c. prophet
   d. servant

4. Jesus was obedient to God the Father even to the point of death on a cross.
   True
   False

5. According to Philippians, Jesus is the name above every other name.

   True

   False

6. Philippians 3:20 says that Christians' citizenship is in

   _____.

   a. heaven
   b. their church
   c. God's kingdom
   d. service to others

● COLOSSIANS

1. Who wrote the letter to the Colossians?
   a. Paul
   b. Apollos
   c. Timothy
   d. A and C

2. Colossians 3:18 instructs wives to love their husbands and do not be harsh with them.
   True
   False

3. Who took this letter to the Colossians?
   a. Titus
   b. Philemon
   c. Tychicus and Onesimus
   d. Paul and Timothy

4. Colossians 3:23 says that whatever we do, we should work at it with all our heart, as working for _____.
   a. our family
   b. the Lord
   c. the church
   d. human masters

5. The book of Colossians commands fathers not to provoke their children to anger so they won't be discouraged.
   True
   False

1 AND 2 THESSALONIANS

1. Thessalonica was a city of _____ culture.
   a. Greek
   b. Turkish
   c. Roman
   d. Babylonian

2. "The wrath to come" in 1 Thessalonians 1:10 refers to
   _____.
   a. judgment day
   b. hell
   c. nuclear war
   d. economic disaster

3. The Thessalonian church was under persecution. Paul said those persecuting the Thessalonian church would be
   _____.
   a. tried and convicted of heresy
   b. punished with everlasting destruction
   c. judged more harshly than the worst of criminals
   d. given prominent places in the city hierarchy

4. Paul said that prior to the end times, Satan will give a "lawless one" the power to perform counterfeit miracles, but Jesus will overthrow and destroy him.

   True

   False

5. What was Paul's side occupation?
   a. moneylender
   b. shepherd
   c. fisherman
   d. tentmaker

6. Paul's motto about work was "If a man will not work, he shall not _____."
   a. receive a paycheck
   b. support his family
   c. eat
   d. be part of the church

7. Paul writes in 1 Thessalonians 4:3 that it is God's will for the Thessalonians to abstain from divorce.

   True

   False

8. 1 Thessalonians 4:16 says Jesus will return from heaven with _____.

    a.   a shout

    b.   the voice of the archangel

    c.   the trumpet of God

    d.   All of the above

● 1 AND 2 TIMOTHY

1. The book of 1 Timothy was a letter from _____ to _____.

   a. Timothy; Paul

   b. Paul; Timothy

   c. Timothy; Corinth

   d. Paul; many Christian leaders

2. According to 2 Timothy 3:16, all Scripture is _____.

   a. edifying to read

   b. important in the Christian life

   c. blessed by God

   d. inspired (breathed) by God

3. How are Christians to endure hardship?

   a. by seeking the power to endure

   b. by believing God will end it soon

   c. by being good soldiers

   d. by being meek lambs

4. The book of 1 Timothy was penned in AD 62 to 66.
   True
   False

5. Who is the one mediator between God and man, according to 1 Timothy 2:5?
   a. Jesus Christ
   b. the Holy Spirit
   c. A and B
   d. None of the above

● TITUS

1. Which of the following is not one of the qualifications Titus lists for elders of the church?
   a. faithful to one wife
   b. blameless
   c. self-controlled
   d. fluent in Greek

2. Titus 1:1 indicates that _____ wrote the book of Titus.
   a. Paul
   b. Peter
   c. Timothy
   d. Silas

3. The author wrote the book of Titus specifically to Titus.
   True
   False

4. Titus 2:11 says, "The grace of God has appeared, bringing salvation for _____."
   a. the Jews
   b. all people
   c. the Gentiles
   d. Christians

5. Titus 3:10 commands that, after warning a person who stirs up division once and then twice, have nothing more to do with him…he is self-condemned.
   True
   False

● PHILEMON

1. Who cared for Paul while the apostle was in prison?

    a. the Romans

    b. the Corinthian church

    c. Onesimus

    d. Philemon

2. Who wrote the book of Philemon?

    a. Paul

    b. Timothy

    c. A and B

    d. Philemon

3. Who is a prisoner for Jesus Christ, as described in Philemon 1:1?

    a. Onesimus

    b. Philemon

    c. Timothy

    d. Paul

4. How many verses are found in the book of Philemon?

    a. 20

    b. 25

    c. 30

    d. 35

5. Epaphras was also a prisoner in Jesus Christ, according to Philemon 1:23.

   True

   False

● HEBREWS

1. Hebrews 3:3–6 says Jesus has been found worthy of greater honor than which Old Testament prophet?
   a. Abraham
   b. Moses
   c. David
   d. Elisha

2. Hebrews 6:19–20 says Jesus entered the depths of hell on humankind's behalf.
   True
   False

3. _____ is being sure of what we hope for and certain of what we do not see, according to Hebrews 11:1.
   a. Faith
   b. Love
   c. Heaven
   d. Discernment

4. Hebrews 13:5 quotes Jesus saying, "I will never leave you nor _____ you."
   a. stop loving
   b. give up on
   c. forget about
   d. forsake

5. Hebrews ends with a verse about Jesus's character, reliability, and eternal nature: "Jesus Christ is the same yesterday and today and _____."

   a. tomorrow

   b. as long as the earth endures

   c. forever

   d. years to come

JAMES

1. James was the brother of _____.
   a. Matthew
   b. Jesus
   c. John
   d. John the Baptist

2. James is considered by many the _____ of the New Testament.
   a. most important book
   b. jewel
   c. Proverbs
   d. most poetic book

3. James says faith without good works is _____.
   a. dead
   b. incomplete
   c. still valuable
   d. faith alone

4. James 1:22 challenges believers to be doers of God's Word and not _____.
   a. hypocrites
   b. lazy
   c. prideful
   d. hearers only

5. James 1:17 says every good gift and every perfect gift in our lives is _____.
   a. to be cherished
   b. earned through good works
   c. through faith alone
   d. from above

✸ 1 AND 2 PETER

1. 1 Peter 2:24 summarizes the gospel: "He himself bore our sins in his _____ on the _____, that we might die to sin and live to righteousness. By his wounds you have been healed."
    a. body; tree
    b. love; cross
    c. pain; cross
    d. blood; mount

2. 1 Peter 5:7 tells Christians to cast all their cares upon God because he cares for them.
    True
    False

3. 1 Peter 5:13 indicates that Peter was in _____ when he wrote 1 Peter.
    a. Jerusalem
    b. Syria
    c. Babylon
    d. Bethlehem

4. Peter commands Christians to _____ in the true grace of God.

    a. stand fast

    b. share

    c. love others

    d. encourage others

5. 2 Peter 3:8 says that, with the Lord, one day is as a thousand years, and a thousand years as one day.

   True

   False

● 1, 2, AND 3 JOHN

1. 1 John 4:8 says that God is _____.
   a. love
   b. good
   c. faithful
   d. almighty

2. What will happen to believers when Christ is revealed, according to 1 John 3?
   a. They will praise and thank God.
   b. They will be like Christ.
   c. They will be born again.
   d. They will be judged.

3. 1 John 1:8 says, "If we say we have no sin, we _____ ourselves, and the truth is not in us."
   a. confuse
   b. deceive
   c. ridicule
   d. forsake

4. 1 John 1:9 says if we confess our sins, Christ will forgive our sins and cleanse us from all _____.
   a. guilt
   b. shame
   c. tribulation
   d. unrighteousness

5. The shortest book in the Bible is 3 John.
   True
   False

✸ JUDE

1. In the opening verse, Jude describes himself as a servant of Jesus Christ and a brother of _____.
   a. Peter
   b. Stephen
   c. John
   d. James

2. How many chapters are in Jude?
   a. 1
   b. 2
   c. 3
   d. 4

3. Who saved the Israelite people out of the land of Egypt?
   a. God
   b. Jesus
   c. Moses
   d. Joshua

4. Sodom and Gomorrah are the two cities specifically mentioned in Jude 1:7 as undergoing a punishment of eternal fire.
   True
   False

5. The last word in the book of Jude is "amen."

   True

   False

● REVELATION

1. Who wrote the book of Revelation?
   a. Paul
   b. John
   c. Stephen
   d. Luke

2. Where was the book of Revelation written from?
   a. Rome
   b. Ephesus
   c. Island of Patmos
   d. Jerusalem

3. Revelation states that anyone whose name was not written in heaven's book of life would be _____.
   a. thrown into the lake of fire
   b. banned from approaching God's heavenly throne
   c. paid penitence for his sins
   d. received a second chance at winning God's favor

4. A sharp, two-edged sword comes out of Jesus's mouth and seven angels rest in his hand in his first appearance in Revelation.
   True
   False

5. Revelation is the last book of the Bible.

   True

   False

New Testament Answer Keys

MATTHEW—ANSWERS

1. C (See Matthew 1:23)
2. D (See Matthew 4:1–11)
3. A (See Matthew 7:24–27)
4. B (See Matthew 11:28)
5. C (See Matthew 11:30)
6. A (See Matthew 13:31)
7. True
8. B
9. D (See Matthew 1:18–19)
10. True (See Matthew 1:18–24)
11. D (See Matthew 9:9)
12. C (See Matthew 2:13–14)
13. D (See Matthew 2:13)
14. False (in the form of a dove; see Matthew 3:17)
15. A (See Matthew 3:13–17)
16. D (See Matthew 14:1–10)
17. B (See Matthew 14:13–21)

18. C (See Matthew 4:2)

19. A (See Matthew 26:15)

20. B (See Matthew 26:15)

21. True (See Matthew 26:51)

22. C (See Matthew 26:69–75)

23. A (See Matthew 27:45)

24. False (The temple curtain split; see Matthew 27:51)

25. B (See Matthew 27:54)

26. D (See Matthew 27:5)

27. False (least popular)

28. A (See Matthew 18:21–22)

29. True (See Matthew 22:37–40)

MARK—ANSWERS

1. B (See Mark 1:9)

2. True (See Mark 1:11)

3. D (See Mark 1:19)

4. C (See Mark 4:38)

5. A (See Mark 4:39)

6. False (She was in her home; see Mark 5)

7. B (See Mark 7:33)

8. C (See Mark 6:14)

9. False (cousin)

10. D (See Mark 1:16–18)

11. B (See Mark 1:6)

12. A (See Mark 1:19)

13. C (See Mark 2:4)

14. B (See Mark 2:27)
15. C (See Mark 3:16–19)
16. True (See Mark 3:22)
17. D (See Mark 4:30–31)
18. A (See Mark 5:1–13)
19. B (See Mark 6:4)
20. C (See Mark 6:43)
21. True (See Mark 6:49)
22. A (See Mark 8:22–25)
23. D
24. D (See Mark 9:2–4)
25. False (It belongs to people who have childlike faith in Christ, "such as these" children that Jesus was with; see Mark 10:14)
26. C
27. A
28. False (Isaiah; see Mark 1:2)
29. B
30. A (See Mark 8:34)
31. C (See Mark 16:8)

LUKE—ANSWERS

1. B
2. D (See Luke 1:26)
3. True (See Luke 1:34)
4. C (See Luke 1:46). This song is known as the "Magnificat."
5. A (See Luke 2:25, 36)
6. D (See Luke 2:52)

7. C (See Luke 3:4)

8. C (See Luke 3:16)

9. B (See Luke 4:17)

10. A (See Luke 4:34)

11. D (See Luke 5:8)

12. C (See Luke 5:18)

13. B (See Luke 5:31)

14. A (See Luke 6:12–16)

15. B (See Luke 6:35)

16. True (See Luke 1:1–4)

17. C (See Luke 2:8–14)

18. B

19. D (See Luke 2:12)

20. False (He was circumcised; see Luke 2:21)

21. A (See Luke 2:39)

22. C (See Luke 3:23)

23. D (See Luke 3:23–38)

24. False (He charged him to tell no one; see Luke 5:14)

25. B (See Luke 6:20–23)

26. B (See Luke 8:1–3)

27. C (See Luke 10:25–37)

28. True (See Luke 8:21)

29. D (See Luke 14:1–6)

30. B (See Luke 17:11–19)

JOHN—ANSWERS

1. C (See John 1:14)
2. B (See John 4:7)
3. B (See John 18:1). This brook is mentioned only in John's gospel.
4. C (See John 1:29)
5. True (See John 1:42)
6. A (See John 2:1–11)
7. D (See John 3:3)
8. D (See John 3:1)
9. False (Jesus offered her living water; see John 4:10)
10. D (See John 5:5)
11. C (See John 6:9)
12. True (See John 6:35)
13. A (See John 8:11)
14. B (See John 9:1–12)
15. C
16. A (See John 11:17)
17. True (See John 11:45–57)
18. C (See John 12:14)
19. D (See John 14:6)
20. False (He washed all the disciples' feet; see John 13:1–12)
21. B (See John 13:38)
22. D (See John 14:15–26)
23. D (See John 17)
24. True (See John 15:1)
25. B (See John 18:1–12)

26. A (See John 19:16)
27. True (See John 19:17)
28. C (See John 19:19)
29. D (See John 19:25–26)
30. B (See John 19:30)
31. C (See John 19:23–24)
32. A (See John 19:38)
33. True (See John 20:1–2)
34. A (See John 20:2–3)
35. False (Mary Magdalene was the first; see John 20:11–18)
36. D (See John 20:19–20)
37. B (See John 20:24)
38. True (See John 20:27)
39. C (See John 20:28)
40. D (See John 20:31)

ACTS—ANSWERS

1. A (See Acts 2:1–4)
2. D (See Acts 18:2–3)
3. True (See Acts 17:10–12)
4. D (See Acts 1:8)
5. B (See Acts 9:3)
6. C
7. True (See Acts 1:1–3)
8. C (See Acts 8:1)
9. B (See Acts 2:41)
10. D (See Acts 9:3)

11. D (See Acts 1:12–26)

12. False (They didn't raise people from the dead; see Acts 2:1–4)

13. A (See Acts 28)

14. C (See Acts 12:7)

15. False (They answered, "We must obey God rather than men"; see Acts 5:29)

ROMANS—ANSWERS

1. B

2. False (everyone who believes; see Romans 1:16)

3. D

4. B (See Romans 1:17)

5. A

6. True

7. D

8. C

9. True (See Romans 1:8–10)

10. B

11. D

12. False (all authority; see Romans 13:1)

13. A (See Romans 4:15–18)

14. True

15. A

1 AND 2 CORINTHIANS—ANSWERS

1. B

2. D (See 1 Corinthians 15:26)

3. True (See 1 Corinthians 13:13)
4. B (See 2 Corinthians 11:25)
5. C (See 2 Corinthians 8:7)

GALATIANS—ANSWERS

1. C (See Galatians 4:7)
2. B
3. C (See Galatians 5:14)
4. True (See Galatians 3:26)
5. D (See Galatians 5:22–23)

EPHESIANS—ANSWERS

1. B (See Ephesians 1:1)
2. C
3. A
4. False (Anointed One)
5. D

PHILIPPIANS—ANSWERS

1. C (See Philippians 2:12)
2. B
3. D
4. True (See Philippians 2:8)
5. True (See Philippians 2:9–10)
6. A

COLOSSIANS—ANSWERS

1. D
2. False (Wives, submit to your husbands, as is fitting in the Lord; see Colossians 3:18)
3. C (See Colossians 4:7)
4. B
5. True (See Colossians 3:21)

1 AND 2 THESSALONIANS—ANSWERS

1. C
2. A
3. B (See 2 Thessalonians 1:9–10)
4. True (See 2 Thessalonians 2:8–10)
5. D
6. C (See 2 Thessalonians 3:10)
7. False (The verse says abstaining from sexual immorality is God's will.)
8. D

1 AND 2 TIMOTHY—ANSWERS

1. B
2. D
3. C (See 2 Timothy 2:3)
4. True
5. A

TITUS—ANSWERS

1. D (See Titus 1:6–9)
2. A
3. True (See Titus 1:4)
4. B
5. True

PHILEMON—ANSWERS

1. C (See Philemon 1:13)
2. C (See Philemon 1:1)
3. D
4. B
5. True

HEBREWS—ANSWERS

1. B
2. False (It says he entered the inner sanctuary behind the temple curtain.)
3. A
4. D
5. C

JAMES—ANSWERS

1. B
2. C
3. A (See James 2:17)

4. D
5. D

1 AND 2 PETER—ANSWERS

1. A
2. True
3. C
4. A
5. True

1, 2, AND 3 JOHN—ANSWERS

1. A
2. B (See 1 John 3:2)
3. B
4. D
5. True

JUDE—ANSWERS

1. D (See Jude 1:1)
2. A
3. B (See Jude 1:5)
4. True
5. True (See Jude 1:25)

REVELATION—ANSWERS

1. B (See Revelation 1:1–2)
2. C (See Revelation 1:9)

3. A (See Revelation 20:15)
4. False (Seven stars are in his hand; see Revelation 1:16)
5. True

Sources

English Standard Version (ESV). *The Holy Bible*, English Standard Version, Copyright 2001 by Crossway Bibles, a division of Good News Publishers.

www.bible.org

www.biblica.com

www.biblegateway.com

www.insight.org

www.funtrivia.com

www.gotquestions.org

www.biblecharts.org

www.encyclopedia.com

www.biblehub.com

www.foxnews.com/us/2012/04/18/state-bible-2012/

www.wycliffe.org/about/why

www.superbibletrivia.com

www.quiz.christiansunite.com

www.biblepath.com

www.answersingenesis.org

www.doinggood.org

www.godsgrazingfield.net

www.amazingfacts.org

www.guinnessworldrecords.com/records-1/best-selling-book-of
-non-fiction/

Recommended Resources

INTERESTED IN GAINING A BETTER understanding of the Bible? Here are some biblically related books that you may find helpful as you read or study the Scriptures yourself. Each book can be found and purchased online or at your local bookstore or library.

Context: How to Understand the Bible
AUTHOR: JAMES NICODEM
Publisher: Moody Publishers
Nicodem's book is designed to teach you how to understand verses and passages using both basic Bible study techniques as well as more in-depth practices.

Understanding the Bible
AUTHOR: JOHN STOTT
Publisher: Zondervan Publishing Company
Get answers to foundational questions about the Bible, such as who wrote the Bible and what its message is, and gain a stronger understanding of Jesus Christ.

30 Days to Understanding the Bible

AUTHOR: MAX ANDERS

Publisher: Thomas Nelson Publishers

This guide uses exercises and anecdotes to teach you essential biblical teachings, as well as information about ancient times geography and core places, events, and people of the Bible, through a fifteen-minute-a-day, thirty-day plan of action.

Hearing God

AUTHOR: DALLAS WILLARD

Publisher: InterVarsity Press

Get answers to the age-old question of how precisely God speaks to you through his written word.

How to Read the Bible for All Its Worth

AUTHORS: GORDON D. FEE, DOUGLAS STUART

Publisher: Zondervan

One of the most popular books for helping readers glean life-changing truths out of their daily Bible readings.

Shaped by the Word

AUTHOR: M. ROBERT MULHOLLAND JR.

Publisher: Upper Room

This book offers a fresh approach to Bible reading designed to spiritually form a biblical world view and values in your heart and mind.

Eat This Book
AUTHOR: EUGENE PETERSON

Publisher: Eerdmans

Peterson's book is for readers who want Bible reading, combined with prayer, to be tools that give them a close and intimate relationship with God.

How to Read the Bible Book by Book: A Guided Tour
AUTHORS: GORDON D. FEE, DOUGLAS STUART

Publisher: Zondervan

This is a Bible survey that walks you through the Scriptures, helping you understand each individual book of the Bible while also showing you how each story and truth fits into Scripture's overall narrative.

Index

O

P

W

Z